100 Years of
Horse Racing
Twentieth Century in Pictures

AMMONITE
PRESS

PRESS
ASSOCIATION
Images

First Published 2009 by
Ammonite Press
an imprint of AE Publications Ltd,
166 High Street, Lewes, East Sussex BN7 1XU

Text copyright Ammonite Press
Images copyright Press Association Images
Copyright in the work Ammonite Press

ISBN 978-1-906672-32-4

Editor: Richard Wiles
Series Editor: Paul Richardson
Picture research: Press Association Images
Design: Gravemaker + Scott

Colour reproduction by GMC Reprographics
Printed by Kyodo Nation Printing Services

Page 2: Technological
changes on the cusp, as a
horse drawn coach and a
motorbus arrive at Epsom for
The Derby race meeting.
4th June, 1913

Page 5: In the St Leger at
Doncaster, *Commanche Run*
ridden by Lester Piggott (R)
wins from *Baynoun* ridden by
Steve Cauthen (L).
15th September, 1984

Page 6: A very close race
as Ted Durcan and *Madame
Trop Vite* (L) win The
Polypipe Flying Childers
Stakes from *Anglezarke*
(C) and *Mythical Border* (R)
during The National Express
Doncaster Cup meeting.
12th September, 2008

100 Y

Ho   **ing**

Twen   **ctures**

Introduction

Horse racing has been a passion of the British since the first meeting at a horse fair in Smithfield, London in 1174. It is known as 'the sport of kings' with good reason: royalty championed it from the outset and has been influential in breeding the bloodstock, which Henry VIII even passed laws to govern. The late Queen Mother was passionate about steeplechasers – her stables produced 400 National Hunt triumphs – while her daughter Queen Elizabeth has a fondness for flat racing, and a stable of breeding mares at Sandringham. One of the highlights of the modern racing calendar, and a major event in the British social whirl, is Royal Ascot. Europe's best-attended race meeting, it attracts more than 300,000 people each year. News interest in Royal Ascot's fashions and attendance by celebrities frequently eclipses coverage of the actual racing.

This does not mean that the sport is the sole domain of royalty. Each season hundreds of thousands of ordinary punters congregate at Britain's 60 racecourses to study form at the paddock alongside experts, clamour at the bookies to steal the best odds, wager a modest amount, break even – or perhaps scoop a big win. By the late 1800s the first licensed racecourses had opened, allowing racing to become a major public spectator sport with races such as the arduous Grand National, which has been run annually at Aintree Racecourse, Liverpool since its inception in 1837, save for five years during the Second World War.

The personalities who populate racing have always intrigued, from notable riders such as Sir Gordon Richards, the greatest ever jockey; Bob Champion, who beat cancer to win the Grand National on *Aldiniti*, a horse threatened with retirement after injury; and Lester Piggott, talented former Queen's jockey jailed for tax irregularities; to the exuberant Italian Frankie Dettori whose 'flying dismounts' thrilled onlookers. However, it is the famous horses that capture the public's imagination: *Arkle*, the greatest steeplechaser of all time; plucky grey *Desert Orchid*, adored for his gritty determination; *Red Rum*, the gelding whose unmatched treble National wins of the 1970s earned him celebrity status, and *Shergar*, acclaimed Derby winner kidnapped by the IRA.

The photographers of the Press Association have been there to record the horses, jockeys, owners, tipsters and punters from the beginning. Through photographs from the PA's vast archives, this book portrays a century of racing and reveals how little the sport has changed: winning or losing remains a finely honed partnership between horse and rider.

Signorinetta, owned and trained by Edoardo Ginistrelli, wins the Epsom Derby Stakes, valued at 6,500 sovereigns, with Billy Bullock in the saddle. *Signorinetta* won the race as a 100–1 rank outsider and became only the fourth filly to win the race – indeed only two fillies have done so since.

1st June, 1908

Signorinetta, with jockey Billy Bullock, being led into the winner's enclosure after winning the Epsom Derby. Incredibly, two days later she won the Oaks

1st June, 1908

100 Years of Horse Racing • Twentieth Century in Pictures

Facing page: A great crowd converges upon *Minoru*, with jockey Herbert Jones in the saddle, as he is led into the winner's enclosure by his owner King Edward VII, after coming home first in the Epsom Derby.
2nd June, 1909

King Edward VII with his horse *Minoru*, the Derby Stakes winner. *Minoru* was the first Derby winner owned by a reigning monarch, although two of the King's horses had previously won the race when he was the Prince of Wales.
1st September, 1909

Facing page: A flurry of activity as punters rush to place their bets with the bookmakers at The Derby.
1st May, 1910

A scene at The Derby, prior to the race commencing. The two-day festival of horse racing began in 1780 at the course located between Epsom, Tadworth and Langley Vale in Surrey. Due to the public nature of the venue people could watch for free, making it one of the most attended sporting events of the year.
1st June, 1910

Lord Villiers' *Greenback*, grazing at Ascot. His Lordship was keen on racing, for some years Senior Steward of the Jockey Club and kept a large stud at Middleton Stoney, Oxfordshire. Unfortunately, his best horse *Greenback* only managed second place in The Derby of 1910.

1st June, 1910

Lomborg, winner of The Derby with jockey Bernard Dillon in the saddle, is led into the winner's enclosure. *Lemberg* started as favorite at 7–4 and was trained by Alec Taylor Jr.
1st June, 1910

Countess Wedell and the
Earl of Portarlington parade
on Royal Day at Ascot
racecourse.
1st August, 1910

If the excitement of a win proved too much, there was always the trusty cycle ambulance to whisk the afflicted away from the bustle of the racecourse.
1911

A thundering start to the
Grand National at Aintree,
Liverpool. *Glenside* won
the race with jockey Jack
Anthony in the saddle.
21st March, 1911

The favourite *Sunstar*, a brown colt owned by the South African mine magnate J B Joel, won the Coronation Derby at Epsom at a canter, defeating the largest field of competitors that had turned out since *Hermit*'s victory in 1867.

3rd June, 1911

The Grand National Cup.
1st March, 1912

Facing page: Mr J B Joel leading in *Jest*, the winner of the Oaks, ridden by Fred Rickaby Jr at Epsom Racecourse. Joel, son of an East End publican, emigrated to South Africa and became a millionaire. Returning to England he controlled mines, breweries and collieries in South Africa, and dealt in gold and diamonds. Extremely successful at racing and breeding, his horses won many of the major contests in the racing calendar.
14th May, 1913

Leading in *Craganour*, ridden
by John Reiff, at The Derby,
Epsom.
1st June, 1913

On Derby Day, a Pearly
King and his family head
for Epsom in their donkey-
hauled trap.
1st June, 1913

Facing page: Mr Taylor leading in *Drinmore* after winning The City and Suburban at Epsom.
1st June, 1913

Craganour, ridden by John Reiff, at The Derby, Epsom.
1st June, 1913

The 6–4 favourite *Craganour* (L), Johnny Reiff in the saddle, beats 100–1 outsider *Aboyeur*, ridden by Edwin Piper, by a head to win The Derby Stakes, only to be disqualified for bumping. He was later sold to Argentina and became a successful sire there.
4th June, 1913

The King's horse *Anmer*, ridden by Herbert Jones during the parade prior to The Derby. During the race a Suffragette, Miss Emily Davison, threw herself under the horse and died later from her injuries. The jockey was injured but later recovered.
4th June, 1913

Facing page: Suffragette
Emily Davison throws herself
under King George V's horse
Anmer at the Epsom Derby.
4th June, 1913

Jockey Herbert Jones is carried
away on a stretcher with mild
concussion and a fractured rib,
after Suffragette Emily Davison
had thrown herself in front of
his horse, *Anmer,* during the
Epsom Derby.
4th June, 1913

Horses and riders pour over
the water jump during the
Grand National at Aintree.
1st April, 1914

Facing page: The Pearly
King of Hoxton (R),
accompanied by two Pearly
Princes and a Pearly
Princess, on the course at
The Derby.
1st June, 1914

A general view of the crowds at The Derby. The race was
won by the American H B Duryea's *Durbar II*, ridden by
Matt MacGee, whose chances of winning were rated at
100–6 against.

1st June, 1914

Firm favourite, Sir John Thuroby's *Kennymore*, with *Black Jester* behind, heads towards the starting line at The Derby.

1st June, 1914

Derby winner *Gay Crusader*, with Steve Donoghue in the saddle. He became the 12th Triple Crown winner in UK history by winning the 2,000 Guineas, The Derby and the St Leger Stakes in 1917, and went on to win the Ascot Gold Cup in the same year.
1st June, 1917

World Flyweight boxing
champion Jimmy Wilde (L)
chats with champion jockey
Steve Donoghue at Windsor
Racecourse.
8th April, 1919

The racecourse at Lincoln, which dates back to 1773. Its March meeting was a popular curtain raiser for the flat racing season, but the venue closed during the Second World War and never regained its prestige. Plans are afoot to restore the course by 2013.

1919

The start of The Derby at Epsom. After commencing in
1779, the race was relocated to Newmarket in 1915, where
it was contested as the New Derby Stakes until 1918. In
1919 the race was returned to its Epsom Downs site and has
remained there ever since.
1st June, 1919

Leading flat race jockey, Steve Donoghue. He was Champion Jockey ten times between 1914 and 1923 and was one of the most celebrated horse racing sportsmen after Fred Archer, arguably only Sir Gordon Richards eclipsing him.
24th October, 1919

Steeplechase jockey Keith Piggott, father of renowned flat race jockey Lester, and one of a dynasty of successful jockeys.
1st March, 1920

Spion Kop wins from *Archaic* and *Orpheus* at The Derby, Epsom, ridden by American jockey Frank O'Neill of St Louis in his first ever Derby win. O'Neill, who rode for William K Vanderbilt on French turf, modestly told newspapermen on alighting the train in Paris: *"Don't quote me on saying that Spion Kop is the best horse I ever rode."*
2nd June, 1920

Facing page: The Prince of Wales (C) with the Duke of York (far L) and Prince Henry (far R) at Sandown Park Races.
12th March, 1921

Facing page: A crowd of 200,000 congregated at Aintree for the Grand National. The arrival of the King and Queen in the Royal Box was greeted with enthusiastic cheers.
19th March, 1921

Sir Malcolm McAlpine's *Shaun Spadah*, ridden by Fred Rees, wins the Grand National. The gelding was the only horse not to fall during the race. Three others out of 35 runners also finished the course after being remounted.
19th March, 1921

King George V congratulates Fred Rees, who rode *Shaun Spadah,* winner of the National. The horse's unusual name is 1920s Cockney rhyming slang for 'car'.
19th March, 1921

The Prince of Wales clears
the Open Ditch in fine style
during his first ride under
National Hunt rules.
1st April, 1921

Hats are raised in salute and the crowd cheers Edward,
Prince of Wales as he enters the enclosure having won the
Harthorn Hill Steeplechase at Sandown Park, Surrey.
1st April, 1921

The start of The Derby Stakes at Epsom Racecourse, known colloquially as 'The Derby'. One of the most prestigious flat races in the world, The Derby is one of the five British Classic Races open to three year old colts and fillies.

1st June, 1921

Humorist (second L), Steve Donoghue in the saddle, comes home to win The Derby by a neck from the 2,000 Guineas winner *Craig an Eran*. Although the winner of four races at two and three years, *Humorist*'s health was delicate, and sadly the chestnut died in his box just two weeks after the race pictured following a massive haemorrhage of the lungs.
1st June, 1921

Polemarch, ridden by Joe Childs, wins the St Leger Stakes at Doncaster. Run over a distance of one mile, six furlongs and 132 yards it is the oldest of the five British Classic Races and also the final leg of both the colts' and fillies' Triple Crowns.
8th September, 1921

Peter Gilpin rides out to superintend the working of his horses. Gilpin was champion trainer in 1904 and 1915, and coached the fabulous mare *Pretty Polly* to win 22 of her 24 starts, *Spearmint*, winner of the 1906 Derby, and *Comrade*, a colt that cost only 25 guineas but went on to win the Grand Prix de Paris and the first running of the Arc de Triomphe. Gilpin built Clarehaven Stables at Newmarket on the betting proceeds of his filly *Clarehaven*, which won the Cesarwitch Handicap of 1900.

23rd May, 1922

The remarkable scene as the runners rounded Tattenham Corner to enter the straight at The Derby. *Captain Cuttle*, ridden by Steve Donoghue, won the race.

31st May, 1922

A general view of Goodwood Racecourse on the South
Downs, near Chichester, from Trundle Hill. Considered to be
one of the most attractive settings for a racecourse its close
proximity to the coast can shroud the racing in fog.
26th July, 1922

Horses and riders leap over the imposing water jump at the Grand National, Aintree. *Sergeant Murphy*, ridden by Captain Tuppy Bennett, became the first American-bred horse to win the Grand National.

23rd March, 1923

Papyrus, with Steve Donoghue in the saddle, winner of the Epsom Derby. Four months later the stallion was shipped to the US with a special feed mix, stablemate *Bargold*, stable cat, two stable boys, his trainer, and jockey Donoghue to participate in a race at Belmont Park, New York against Kentucky Derby winner *Zev*. Racing on a dirt track for the first time, in heavy mud, *Papyrus* was beaten by five lengths, under the gaze of a crowd of some 50,000.

5th June, 1923

All the tension is unleashed
at the start of the Epsom
Derby, as horses and riders
surge forwards.
6th June, 1923

The finish of The Derby showing Lord Derby's *Sansovino* and jockey Thomas Weston racing six lengths clear of *St Germain*, *Hurstwood* and the remainder of the field to win decisively. The going had been muddy after prolonged rain for days beforehand.

4th June, 1924

Facing page: The Earl of Derby leads The Derby Stakes winner, *Sansovino*, through the throng to the unsaddling enclosure.

4th June, 1924

Henry Ternynck's *Massine* winning the Gold Cup at Ascot by a short head from *Filbert de Savoie* with *Inkerman* third.
19th June, 1924

Facing page: The immaculately dressed Prince Henry (C) and his entourage arrive at Royal Ascot.
10th June, 1924

Mr Percy Whitaker (L), trainer of *Silvo*, the horse that came third in the 1924 Grand National, with the horse's owner.
1st March, 1925

Manna, ridden by the universally popular Steve Donoghue, being led into the winner's enclosure after the Epsom Derby. Donoghue had an illustrious career as a flat race jockey, winning The Derby six times, including three consecutive wins in 1921, 1922 and 1923.
31st May, 1925

Facing page: A study of
three notable jockeys (L–R):
Charlie Elliott, Freddie Fox
and Tommy Weston.
1926

Flat race jockey Gordon Richards was Champion Jockey
26 times, winning 14 Classic races. In 1926 Richards
contracted tuberculosis and was obliged to take time off from
racing, although he soon returned to form, displaying his
unconventional riding style – long reins, upright stance with a
slightly twisted torso.
26 September, 1927

The notorious Becher's Brook claims two more victims as a crowd looks on. The fence was named after Captain Martin Becher who, unseated from his mount *Conrad,* fell into the brook that ran along the landing side when leading in 1839. The obstacle was remodelled in 1989 and the brook drained to remove the risk of fallen horses drowning, although purists objected.

30th March, 1928

The start of the 1929 Grand National, showing a record number of starters with 66 horses lined up for the race. The smallest field was in 1883 when just ten horses competed.
22nd March, 1929

Some of the field bravely taking Becher's Brook, sixth obstacle in the Grand National, only to tumble painfully on landing.
22nd March, 1929

Freddie Fox, Champion
Jockey for 1930. Born
in Wiltshire in 1888, Fox
was apprenticed at 18 and
had his first winner just a
year later. He rode for the
prestigious von Weinberg
stable in Germany from
1912 to 1913 but returned
to England prior to the First
World War. When retired
from racing in 1936, he still
weighed a slight 7st 7lb.
1st November, 1929

The Gold Cup at Ascot with
Bosworth leading the field to
give trainer Lord Derby his first
win at this prestigious race.
30th June, 1930

Tom Coulthwaite's *Grakle* (R), wearing number six, Bob Lyall in the saddle, and 1929's winner *Gregalach*, with Robert Everett on board, take the last jump just before the winning post at the Grand National at Aintree. *Grakle* held the lead to win the race.

27th March, 1931

Mr Fred Darling, British thoroughbred racehorse trainer, was Champion Trainer six times, and also trained a record-equalling seven English Derby winners. He took over the Beckhampton stables from his father Sam, also a trainer, on his retirement, and remained there until his own retirement in 1947.

1st June, 1931

The field rounding Tattenham
Corner during The Derby.
1st June, 1932

A crowded scene at
The Derby at Epsom,
as competitors begin to
assemble for the start.
1st June, 1932

Facing page: The field at the half mile stage of the Epsom
Derby. The race was won by *April the Fifth*, at odds of 110–6,
ridden by Fred Lane. The stallion was foaled on the 5th April,
coincidentally his breeder's birthday. He was the last Epsom
Derby winner to be trained at Epsom.
15th July, 1932

Facing page: Mr J Cooper's *Roi de Paris*, ridden by Mr Buckham, wins the Ascot Stakes by a short head from *Loosestrife* and *Dictum*.
13th June, 1933

Hyperion, ridden by Tommy Weston and owned by Edward Stanley, 17th Earl of Derby, was winner of both the 1933 St Leger Stakes and The Derby.
1st May, 1933

Champion British jockey Gordon Richards regarded as one of the world's greatest jockeys, and the only one to be knighted – relaxing with his wife and two sons at Shoreham-on-Sea.

24th July, 1933

Gordon Richards on *Elsenor*,
winning the Mitre Selling
Plate at the Hurst Park
racecourse, to equal Fred
Archer's record.
4th November, 1933

A great little man dwarfed by his police escort. Gordon Richards at Hurst Park Racecourse after riding his 246th winner to equal Fred Archer's record.

4th November, 1933

Southern Hero leading from
Thomond II and *Golden Miller*
at the stands fence during the
Cheltenham Gold Cup.
14th March, 1935

Facing page: *Golden Miller*, ridden by Gerry Wilson, was winner of the Grand National and five times winner of the Cheltenham Gold Cup, the only horse to have won both of the United Kingdom's premier steeplechases in the same year.
1st October, 1934

Windsor Lad, nearest the camera, carrying regular jockey Charlie Smirke, holds off the challenge of *Fair Trial* at the Eclipse Stakes, Sandown Park. The horse had won The Derby and the St Leger Stakes the previous year.
19th July, 1935

Grand National winner *Reynoldstown*, with Fulke Walwyn in the saddle, is led into the winner's enclosure by owner Major Noel Furlong after winning his second successive Grand National.
27th March, 1936

Captain H Allison in his
Epsom clothes, preparing
to start The Derby.
1st June, 1936

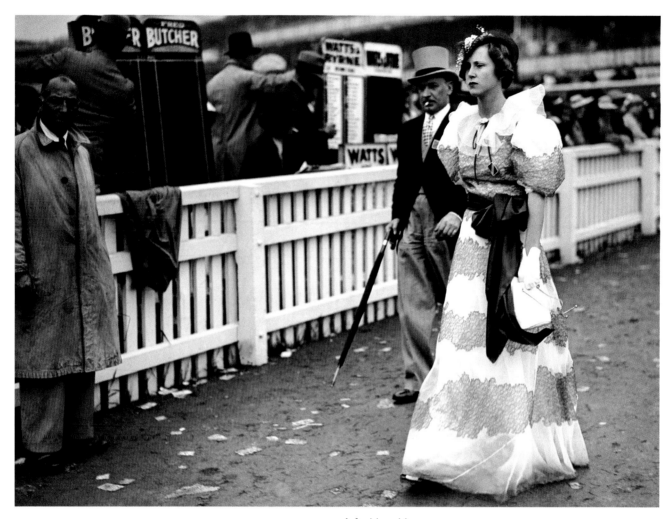

A fashionable young woman
passes bookmakers as she
attends the Royal Ascot
races.
1st June, 1936

Royal Ascot, dating back to 1711, is a major event in the British social calendar, and commands a strict dress code in the Royal Enclosure. Women, for example, must always wear a hat. Press reports on the fashions frequently outweigh those of the actual racing.

15th June, 1936

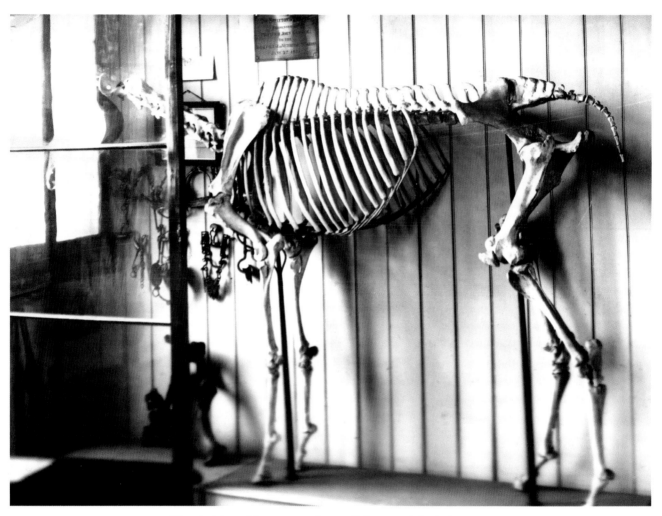

The skeleton of famous racehorse *Eclipse*, undefeated during his entire career which started in 1769, and retired to stud in 1771 due to lack of competition. The stallion sired well over 300 foals and in 1937 The Royal Veterinary College calculated that nearly 80 per cent of modern thoroughbred racehorses have *Eclipse* in their pedigree.
1937

Becher's Brook second time around showing the eventual winner *Royal Mail* and jockey Evan Williams leading the field, ahead of *Flying Minute* and *Delachance*.
24th March, 1937

Spectators use the roof of a train, standing by Becher's
Brook, as a grandstand to watch the Grand National.
24th March, 1937

A riotous view of the bookies and a mass of eager punters at Epsom for The Derby.
1st June, 1937

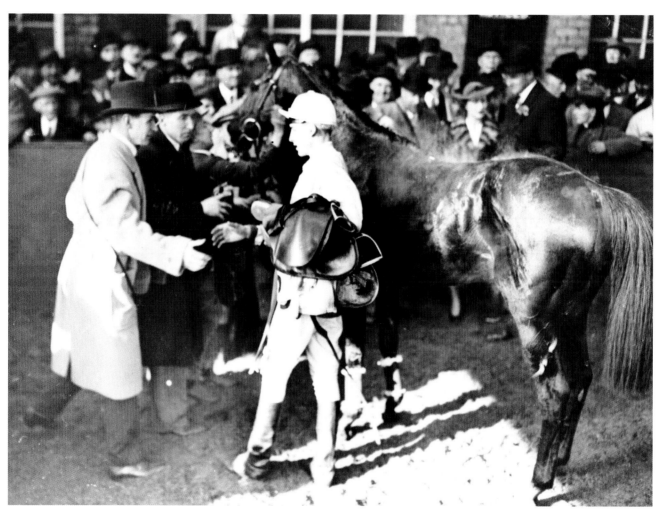

Bruce Hobbs, the 17 year old
winner of the Grand National on
Battleship, being congratulated
by his father. Hobbs was
and still is the youngest-ever
winning jockey.
1st April, 1938

Facing page: *Bois Roussel*
ridden by Charlie Elliott
winning The Derby at Epsom.
1st June, 1938

100 Years of Horse Racing • Twentieth Century in Pictures

Bois Roussel, after winning
the Epsom Derby, was
returned to his stables by train.
6th June, 1938

Gordon Richards glances
over his shoulder as his
mount, *Quartier-Maitre* (R)
passes the post to win the
Lincolnshire Handicap at
Doncaster.
3rd April, 1940

AINTREE SPRING MEETING, 1940
AIR RAID
PRECAUTIONS
If an AIR RAID ALARM is SOUNDED, go to the corrugated iron fence and lie down. Remain there until the 'all clear' is given.
DON'T attempt to leave the Course by Motor Vehicle.
FOLLOW THE INSTRUCTIONS OF THE POLICE AND AIR RAID WARDENS

Facing page: Two racegoers
read a notice informing
punters of the air raid
precautions in place during
the Aintree Spring Meeting.
5th April, 1940

Not even a war would prevent
the British racegoers from
enjoying their sport, as shown
by the packed car park at
Epsom for The Derby.
18th June, 1941

Setting the pace in The Derby (L–R) *Selim Hassan*, *Starwort* and *Annatom*, with the eventual winner *Owen Tudor* barely visible between *Selim Hassan* and *Starwort* (jockey in dark cap).
18th June, 1941

Punters on Ascot Heath
place their bets.
14th June, 1945

100 Years of Horse Racing • Twentieth Century in Pictures

Facing page: Jockey Gordon
Richards wins his 100th race of
the season, the Castle Hill Plate
at Windsor, on *Sez You*.
12th October, 1945

During the Grand National at Aintree, *Bogskar* unseats his
rider at The Chair, the biggest fence in the race. The horse
had won the National in 1940 with jockey Flight Sergeant
Mervyn Jones in the saddle, the last year the race was run
during the war years. Jones was subsequently lost in action
at the age of 22.
5th April, 1946

Largo falling at Becher's Brook during the 1946 Grand National.
5th April, 1946

A general view of the finish
showing *Airborne* leading
from *Gulf Stream* and
Radiotherapy at The Derby
Stakes.
1st June, 1946

A view of Goodwood looking towards Trundle Hill from the stands. Inspection of the horses is taking place in the paddock.

1st July, 1946

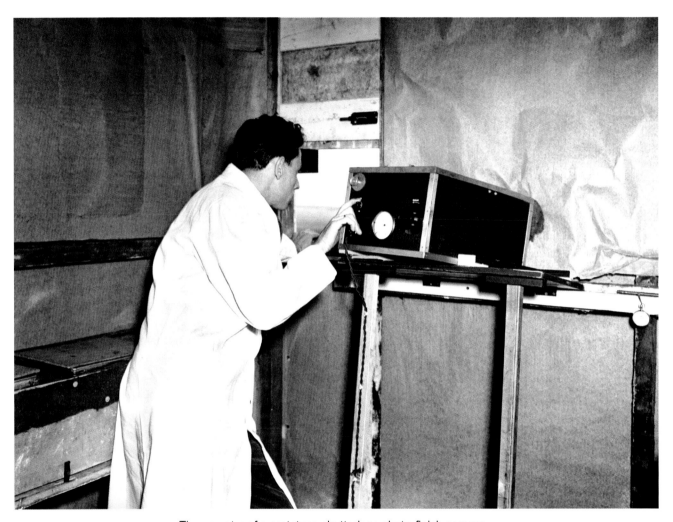

The operator of a prototype shutterless photo-finish camera
waits for the runners to pass in front of him during testing.
The camera is situated in a small dark room in a tower 30ft
high, 80ft from the rails, and 20yd short of the winning post.
An actual race finish is to be used for the final test before the
camera can be installed on racecourses throughout the country.
2nd July, 1946

Plucky *Caughoo* wins the National by a comfortable margin, one of only four winners with odds of 100–1. Rumour held that the horse, concealed by fog, hid behind a fence, emerging near the end of the race to romp home 20 lengths clear of the field. Jockey Eddie Dempsey, accused of cheating, was beaten up in a bar by a fellow jockey. Suspicion marred his career. The truth was revealed when the *Irish Mirror* published photographs of *Caughoo* jumping Becher's Brook on two occasions.
29th March, 1947

Tudor Minstrel, with Gordon
Richards in the saddle,
is led in after winning the
2,000 Guinea Stakes at
Newmarket by eight lengths,
the biggest winning margin
since 1900.
30th April, 1947

Derby race winner *Pearl Diver*, ridden by George Bridgland, is led into the winner's enclosure by his owner Baron Geoffroy de Waldner.

7th June, 1947

King George VI and Queen
Elizabeth drive along the
Royal Ascot course in an
open landau.
12th June, 1947

Stagecoaches being used as
grandstands at Ascot.
19th June, 1947

Jockey W Redmond, who
slipped off *Grand Manner*
on the way to the start at
the Waterside Handicap,
Lingfield Park, left her again
at the open ditch.
19th December, 1947

The winner of the King
George VI Chase at
Kempton Park, Mr A G
Boley's *Rowland Roy*, ridden
by Bryan Marshall, returns to
the scale.
26th December, 1947

At close quarters to the action, spectators witness the horses taking the open ditch at the Chiswick Handicap Steeplechase, Kempton Park.
26th December, 1947

A thundering charge of
hooves as the gun goes off
to start the Grand National.
20th March, 1948

A man riding a small motor scooter – of a type used by airborne troops during the Second World War – at Ascot Racecourse is nevertheless correctly dressed for the occasion.
5th June, 1948

Earth moving machines roll
in to start work on a new
course at Ascot.
1st December, 1948

Facing page: *Cottage Rake*, ridden by Aubrey Brabazon, was winner of the Cheltenham Gold Cup.
11th April, 1949

Russian Hero, ridden by Leo McMorrow, is led into the winner's enclosure after taking first place in the Grand National.
26th March, 1949

Facing page: People placing bets at a 'totalisator' at the Grand National at Aintree. The 'tote board' was a numeric or alphanumeric display conveying the odds or payoffs for each horse, the first manufactured for the horse racing industry by the American Totalizator Company.
25th March, 1950

Freebooter, ridden by Jimmy Power, clears the last fence on his way to winning the Grand National.
25th March, 1950

Facing page: Leader of the Opposition Winston Churchill and his wife Clementine arrive at Ascot for the races.
13th June, 1950

A young lady stands on a post to view The Derby at Epsom.
26th May, 1950

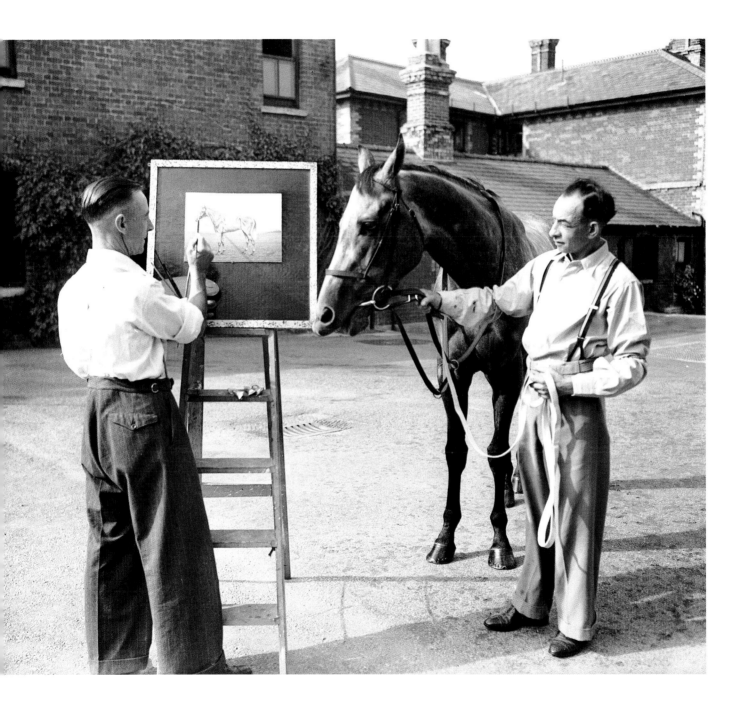

Facing page: Sam Thomas, stable lad, painting racehorse *Palestine*, the winner of the 2,000 Guineas Stakes, at Marcus Marsh's stables.
4th August, 1950

National Spirit (R), D Dillon in the saddle, stumbles and falls at the last fence, allowing *Hatton's Grace* (L), ridden by Tim Molony, to race on and win his third consecutive Champion Hurdle victory at Cheltenham.
6th March, 1951

At the Grand National at Aintree, eventual winner *Nickel Coin* (L), Johnny Bullock in the saddle, and *Gay Heather*, ridden by R Curran, take the 17th fence together.

7th April, 1951

Facing page: Ras Prince Monolulu, famed tipster, offers a Derby hint to policemen at Epsom, Surrey. Real name Peter Carl Mackay from the Caribbean island of St Croix, he was a stalwart of the British horse racing scene from the 1920s until his death in 1965. Noticeable for his flamboyant clothing, he was known for the catchphrase *"I gotta horse"*. In 1920 he had won a bet on The Derby with *Spion Kop*, a 100–6 outsider, earning him the vast sum of £8,000, and became a tipster thereafter.

30th May, 1951

Fancied to beat the French challenge in The Derby at Epsom was the Aga Khan's *Tulyar*. He had won each of the three races he had entered that year: the 2,000 Guineas Trial Stakes (Hurst Park), the Ormonde Stakes (Chester) and The Derby Trial Stakes (Lingfield Park).

23rd May, 1952

Pearly Kings and Queens arrive
at Epsom Racecourse on motor
scooters for Derby Day.
28th May, 1952

Sunbathers watch horse racing at Hurst Park Racecourse, West Molesey in Surrey. The course, laid out in 1890, was the setting for the Triumph Hurdle from 1939 until it closed in 1962, when the land was sold for residential housing.
28th July, 1952

Facing page: The Royal Drive along the course at Ascot.
17th June, 1952

Facing page: *Pinza* (R) ridden by Gordon Richards, races to victory ahead of *Aureole*, ridden by Harry Carr, and *Pink Horse*, with Rae Johnstone in the saddle. After 28 attempts to win The Derby, Richards finally triumphed on his last race on the course.
6th June, 1953

Early Mist, ridden by Bryan Marshall, jumps the last fence on his way to victory in the Grand National at Aintree. Irish trainer Vincent O'Brien coached the winners of the National for three consecutive years in the 1950s, starting with *Early Mist* in 1953, then *Royal Tan* in 1954 and *Quare Times* in 1955.
29th March, 1953

Jockey Derek Ancil is thrown off *Triplc Torch* at The Chair, a fence that is part of the Grand National course. Sited in front of the grandstands it is one of only two fences to be negotiated just once, and is the fifteenth fence in the race. The tallest fence, it measures about 6ft high, with a 5ft 2in open ditch on the take off side and a raised landing side.

27th March, 1954

Facing page; Bookmaker Johnny of Bromley with a patriotic display in the year of Queen Elizabeth II's Coronation.

6th June, 1953

Mr J H Griffin's *Royal Tan*, trained in Ireland by Vincent O'Brien and ridden by Bryan Marshall, won the Grand National at Aintree.

27th March, 1954

Mrs Netta Tudor, wearing an
unconventional hat featuring
a model racehorse, at Royal
Ascot.
15th June, 1954

The Queen smiles and gives her four year old colt *Aureole* a congratulatory pat on the nose after his victory in the King George VI and Queen Elizabeth Stakes at Ascot races.
17th July, 1954

Jockey Fred Winter is
unseated as *Coupar* falls
during the Royal Borough
Handicap Hurdle at Windsor.
7th January, 1955

Leaping over Becher's Brook for the second time are (L–R)
Devon Loch, ridden by Dick Francis, the eventual winner *ESB*,
ridden by Dave Dick, and *Sundew*, ridden by Fred Winter.
24th March, 1956

Dejected jockey Dick Francis is led away after his horse, *Devon Loch*, owned by the Queen Mother, slipped and came to a standstill only 50yd from winning the Grand National.
24th March, 1956

Sundew, ridden by Fred Winter, is led into the winner's enclosure after his success in the Grand National.

27th March, 1957

Sir Winston Churchill watching
his horse *Le Pretendant*, ridden
by S Clayton.
17th May, 1957

Actress Elizabeth Taylor with
husband Mike Todd walking
the course at Epsom.
5th June, 1957

Hot favourite *Crepello* and jockey Lester Piggott proved an
unbeatable combination in The Derby at Epsom, winning
by two lengths. However, tendon problems meant this was
the horse's last race before a career at stud lasting into the
mid-1970s.
5th June, 1957

Racegoers in the grandstand
and Royal Enclosure at
Royal Ascot.
18th June, 1957

The Queen leading in her
Oaks winner filly *Carrozza*
with Lester Piggott in the
saddle, at Epsom.
7th October, 1957

Some have already staked their car-top 'grandstand' seats but
most of the crowd at Epsom just relax on the grass and enjoy
the sunshine while waiting for The Derby to commence.
3rd June, 1959

All the best bloodstock is paraded around the arena at the Newmarket sales, where dealers, trainers and owners congregate to buy and sell potential champions.
1st September, 1959

Facing page: Lester Piggott (R) tries desperately to hang on to *Barbary Pirate*, as he is unseated on the final straight at Brighton.
18th August, 1960

Racehorse plater (light horseshoe maker) Dick Culpin, pictured in his Nottingham workshop where, in readiness for the flat racing season, he is busy making the light alloy plates that are worn by horses for racing.
27th February, 1960

Nicolaus Silver, ridden by
Bobby Beasley, comes home
to win the Grand National.
25th March, 1961

Facing page: A gruesome sight at Becher's Brook the first
time around as *Kingstel*, ridden by George Slack, takes a
nosedive into the turf. The horse hit the fence with his chest,
turned a somersault, and pinned Slack beneath him. The
jockey was merely stunned but his mount broke a shoulder.
25th March, 1961

Ayala, ridden by Pat Buckley
and owned by Keith Piggott,
passes the post to win the
Grand National.
30th March, 1963

Facing page: At least this couple were amused by the rain
as they rushed through mud and puddles from the paddock
at Ascot when the programme was washed out due to heavy
rain. This was the first time in the century that anyone could
recall an entire Royal Ascot programme being lost through
bad weather.
18th June, 1964

Jay Trump (R), Tommy Smith
in the saddle, passes the
post to win from *Freddie* (L),
ridden by Phil McCallan, at
the Grand National.
27th March, 1965

Facing page: *The Rip* (L),
ridden by W Rees and
owned by the Queen Mother,
in action. The horse, an
entry for the Grand National
at Aintree on the 27th of
March 1965, was trained by
Peter Cazalet.
3rd February, 1965

The legendary trainer Tom Dreaper, who won the Cheltenham Gold Cup three times in succession with the great steeplechaser *Arkle* in the mid-1960s.
4th April, 1965

Arkle, with Pat Taaffe in the saddle, leads *Brasher,* ridden by Jimmy Fitzgerald over the last fence before going on to win the Whitbread Gold Cup. Trained by Tom Dreaper in Ireland, *Arkle* was the first racehorse to capture the British and Irish public imagination outside of racing circles, winning 27 of his 35 starts.

24th April, 1965

Facing page: *Sea Bird II*, widely regarded as the greatest post-war European flat race horse, wins the 1965 Derby ridden by Pat Glennon, after a magnificent run. Starting at odds of 7–4 he won by a very easy two lengths from *Meadow Court*.
2nd June, 1965

The Queen Mother pats her horse *Irish Rover* after he won the Marden Novices Hurdle.
8th November, 1965

Trainer Mr Pat Taylor of
Beverley, Yorkshire with
racehorse *Rhumau*.
15th March, 1966

T G Wilkinson's *Flying Boll,* ridden by Pat Taaffe, was winner of the Queen Mother's Champion Chase at Cheltenham Racecourse.

17th March, 1966

Arkle, ridden by Pat Taaffe in his second race of the day, taking the last jump in the Cheltenham Gold Cup at Cheltenham.
17th March, 1966

Anglo (R), ridden by Tim Norman, clears the last fence ahead of *Forest Prince* (L) before sprinting on to win the National.
26th March, 1966

Crowd scene at Ascot Races.
3rd June, 1966

At the water jump of the SGB Handicap Steeplechase Chase the astonishing *Arkle*, ridden by Pat Taaffe and owned by Anne, Duchess of Westminster, leads the field.
14th December, 1966

Arkle gets a 'snifter' at a bottle of Guinness while recovering from a fractured bone in the leg at Kempton. Often known simply as 'Himself', *Arkle* was a legend in Ireland, his strength wryly claimed to come from drinking the famous stout twice a day.
12th January, 1967

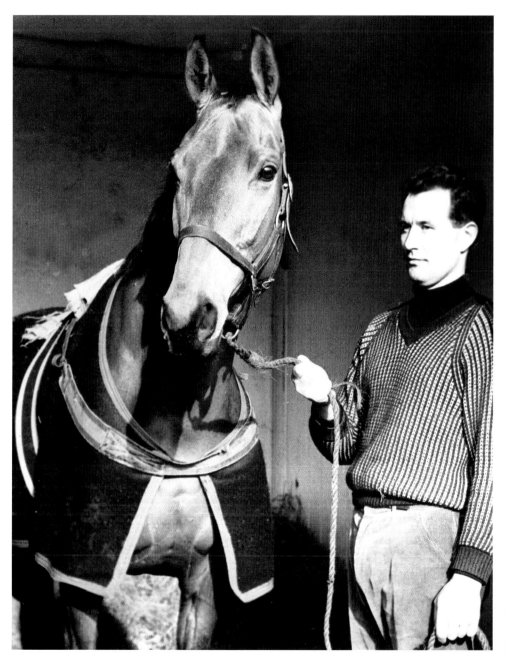

Arkle, who broke a pedal bone in his foot during his final race on the 27th of December 1966, recuperating in his box with trainer Vincent Slevin. He was in plaster for four months and, although recovering, never ran again. Retired and ridden as a hack by his owner he succumbed to arthritis, possibly brucellosis, and was put down at the age of 13.
20th January, 1967

Facing page: Four Grand National entries from Captain Neville Crump's string at Middleham, Yorkshire: (L–R) *Forest Prince* (jockey Pat Buckley), *Limeking* (Frankie Stewart), *Tudor Deal* (Joe Reardon) and *Forecastle* (Derek Hamilton). Frankie, Derek and Joe are stable boys.

25th February, 1967

The 100–1 outsider *Foinavon*, ridden by John Buckingham, takes the last fence to win Aintree's Grand National.

8th April, 1967

Mill House, David Nicholson in the saddle, clears the last fence before going on to win the Whitbread Gold Cup at Sandown.
29th April, 1967

Sporting journalist Peter O'Sullevan goes over the course during a trial run of the first electronic horse race in the world, which will be staged at the University of London.

16th December, 1967

Sir Ivor, ridden by Lester Piggott, is led into the winner's enclosure after prevailing in The Derby.
29th May, 1968

A white-gloved tic tac man signals the odds on Derby Day at Epsom racecourse. Bookies use tic tac to communicate with their staff and ensure that their odds are not too dissimilar to those on their competitors' boards, which situation punters could use to their advantage.

1st June, 1968

The Best family enjoy a
day out at Brighton races:
(L–R) Tony Best, wife Sylvia,
children Damian and Jenisca
– and not forgetting boxer
dog Baron.
7th August, 1969

Studying the form are Vincent (L) and Peter O'Brien. In 2001 Vincent O'Brien was voted the greatest influence in horse racing history, after a poll hosted by *The Racing Post* newspaper. He had a gift for picking world class horses, in particular the use of the bloodline of the Canadian-bred horse *Northern Dancer*, one of whose issues was *Nijinsky*, ridden to victory at Epsom by Lester Piggott. O'Brien trained six horses to win the Epsom Derby and was twice British Champion Trainer.

1st October, 1969

Horses at the start of the flat
racing season, as the tape
goes up for the 'off' at the
First Apprentice Handicap,
Doncaster.
23rd March, 1970

In the Grand National the field takes the water jump the first time around: (L–R) *Assad*, ridden by Josh Gifford leads from *No Justice*, ridden by J Guest, *The Otter* (number 13), ridden by Tim Jones, and the eventual winner *Gay Trip* (number 2), with Pat Taaffe in the saddle.

4th April, 1970

Nijinsky (L), ridden by Lester Piggott, passes the post to win the Epsom Derby. Trained in Ireland by Vincent O'Brien, the imposing, muscular racehorse enjoyed a string of wins that revealed his regular partnership with Piggott as formidable.
3rd June, 1970

Facing page: The band of the Welsh Guards play as they walk up the course, the first time they performed at Epsom.
3rd June, 1970

Nijinsky with Lester Piggott in the saddle, is led in after winning the St Leger Stakes. When he came second in the Prix de l'Arc de Triomphe, Paris, and in his final race, the Champion Stakes, it was apparent that he was past his best and immediately retired, becoming a successful stud who sired 155 winning racehorses.

12th September, 1970

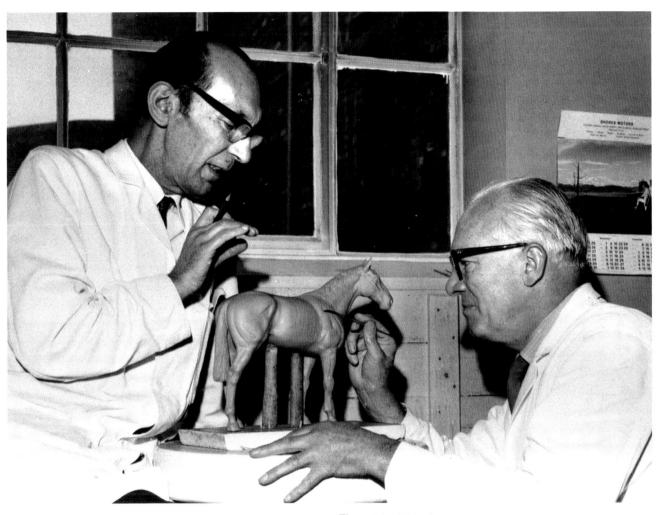

The greatest racehorse of the year, *Nijinsky* being immortalised in pottery by John Beswick Limited, manufacturers of pottery animals for more than 70 years.
16th October, 1970

Jockey Lester Piggot (L), voted among the leading racing personalities of the year, receiving his award from Lord Derby at The Derby Awards luncheon at the Dorchester Hotel, London.
10th December, 1970

Brigadier Gerard, ridden by
Joe Mercer, comes home to
win The 2,000 Guineas at
Newmarket.
2nd May, 1971

Mill Reef, ridden by G Lewis, is led into the winner's enclosure after winning The Derby Stakes at Epsom. His owner Paul Mellon is seen in front of the horse wearing a light top hat.

2nd June, 1971

An enthusiastic *Mill Reef* (R), having his last major work-out
for the Prix de l'Arc de Triomphe at Newbury. His galloping
companions are *Aldie* (second R), and *National Park*.
19th September, 1971

Sir Noel Murless, one of the outstanding trainers of the Classic Thoroughbred in the history of English racing. His record of 19 Classic winners includes three Derbys (*Crepello, St Paddy* and *Royal Palace*). He was also the trainer of *Petit Etoile, Abernant* and *Tudor Minstrel.*

6th April, 1972

Well To Do (R), with Graham Thorner in the saddle, takes the last fence ahead of *Gay Trip* (L), ridden by Terry Biddlecombe, *General Symons* (second L), P Kiely in the saddle, and *Black Secret* (second R), ridden by S Barker.
8th April, 1972

Pendil, ridden by Richard Pitman, sails over the last fence a few lengths ahead of *The Dickler* (second L) ridden by Ron Barry, and *Charlie Potheen* (L) with Terry Biddlecombe in the saddle, winning the Cheltenham Gold Cup.
15th March, 1973

Facing page: A line of open-topped double decker buses gives a commanding view of the track for lucky punters at the Epsom Derby.
9th June, 1972

A thrilling finish to the Grand National Steeplechase at Aintree. *Red Rum*, ridden by Brian Fletcher, swept to a three-quarters length victory and his first National win, over *Crisp,* ridden by Richard Pitman (R), who had led the race nearly all the way.
31st March, 1973

Facing page: *Morston* (second R), Eddie Hide in the saddle, wins The Derby Stakes from *Cavo Doro* (third R), Lester Piggott in the saddle, and *Freefoot* (R), ridden by Pat Eddery. *Morston* was running in only his second race and won at odds of 25–1.
6th June, 1973

An excitable Whitbread Gold Cup winner *Captain Christy*, ridden by Bobby Beasley, is led in to the winner's enclosure at the Cheltenham festival.

14th March, 1974

A photocall for lady jockeys at Kempton Park (L–R back)
Beryl Smith, Cicley Stevens, Gisie Hertzog, Ruth Hegard,
Adriana Piotto, Croci Brooke-Sanders, Suzanne Kane,
Margot Von Pretz, Eva Palyzova, (L–R front) Merial Turnell,
Marycke de Kat, Joy Gibson, Susan Hogan, Ingrid Trautman,
Brita Lundgren, Paula Goyoage.
2nd April, 1974

Jane McDonald, who rode as the first professional female jockey, at Doncaster, makes her way to the weighing room before the race.
20th March, 1975

Looking casual and relaxed despite the inevitable pre-race nerves, five jockeys wait to start the Grand National at Aintree: (L–R) Bill Smith, Jeremy Glover, Jimmy Burke, Ron Berry and Martin Blackshaw.
5th April, 1975

Night Nurse (R), Paddy
Broderick in the saddle,
leads over the last fence
from *Monksfield* (L), who
came second, and *Dramatist*
(C), who came third.
16th March, 1977

Barony Fort, ridden by Charlotte Brew, takes the water jump at the Grand National. At 21 years of age the jockey was the first woman to ride in the National, but never completed the course since her mount – an 18th birthday gift from her parents – decided enough was enough, and pulled up four fences from home.

2nd April, 1977

Facing page: *Red Rum* wins his third Grand National. With Brian Fletcher in the saddle the gelding won in 1973 and 1974, and came second in 1975. Tommy Stack rode him to second place in 1976, and then to victory in 1977.
2nd April, 1977

Red Rum, at trainer Ginger McCain's Southport stable, where the 12 year old was enjoying his return to the quiet life after leaping into National Hunt history with a record third win in the Grand National. A national celebrity, '*Rummy*' made numerous public appearances, his likeness adorned products from mugs, models and posters to jigsaw puzzles, and his life story was the subject of several books.
3rd April, 1977

The Minstrel (L), Lester Piggott in the saddle, puts on a spurt to pip *Hot Grove* (second L), jockeyed by Willie Carson, to the post at The Derby Stakes. The chestnut colt was trained by Vincent O'Brien and owned by the flamboyant Robert Sangster, heir to the Vernons football pools fortune.
1st June, 1977

Sagaro, ridden by Lester Piggott, on his way to winning the Gold Cup at Royal Ascot. He became the first horse to win three Ascot Gold Cups in a row. The challenging race, run over two and a half miles, is the test of a real 'stayer', and chestnut *Sagaro* is regarded as one of the greatest in racing history.

16th June, 1977

The Queen, with long time friend and racing manager Lord Porchester (L) and trainer Ian Balding in the paddock before The Derby, in which her colt *English Harbour* was unplaced. Despite a passion for her racehorses the Queen never bets. Current bloodstock and racing adviser John Warren, who succeeded father-in-law Lord Porchester, reveals that Her Majesty does enjoy a sweepstake: *"On Derby Day, there's one in the Royal Box, and everyone puts in a pound."* The winner gets about £16.

7th June, 1978

In the King George VI Chase at Kempton Park *Jack ot Trumps* (second L) leads from eventual winner *Gay Spartan* (L), *The Champ* and *Royal Frolic*. The Boxing Day race, open to horses aged four or older, is run at Kempton Park over a distance of three miles, including 18 fences.
26th December, 1978

Rough and Tumble (R), Johnny Francome in the saddle, leads *Zongalero* (C), ridden by B R Davies, and eventual winner *Rubstic* (L), with Maurice Barnes in the saddle, over the last fence of the Grand National. The victor, based in Roxburghshire, was the first National winner to be trained in Scotland.

31st March, 1979

Winner of The Epsom
Oaks is *Scintillate*, with
Pat Eddery in the saddle.
The race, first run in 1779,
is a testing course over
one and a half miles of
undulating downland, and is
restricted to three year old
thoroughbred fillies.
9th June, 1979

For the second consecutive year *Le Moss*, Joe Mercer on top (L), wins the Goodwood Cup from *Ardross*, jockeyed by Christy Roche. The race is part of Britain's Stayers' Triple Crown for horses capable of running longer distances. *Le Moss* had a stubborn streak: after an injury he would not leave the yard with anyone but the head lad, frequently refused to gallop, and notably kept fit by swimming.

1st August, 1980

Sea Pigeon (C) with John Francombe in the saddle, on the way to winning his second successive Waterford Crystal Champion Hurdle Challenge Trophy at Cheltenham.
17th March, 1981

Aldaniti, ridden by Bob Champion, races to victory after clearing the last fence of the Grand National. It was a poignant win for the jockey, diagnosed with cancer in 1979, while the racehorse had struggled to overcome a serious injury. *Aldaniti* starred as himself alongside John Hurt in the 1983 film *Champions*, based on the book written by the jockey and Jonathan Powell.
4th April, 1981

NO'S
THE DERBY STKS
1 A.GIBERT
3 W.CARSON
5 J.MATTHIAS
6 P.BRADWELL
7 G.STARKEY
8 S.CAUTHEN
9 B.TAYLOR
18

Shergar, the bay colt owned by a syndicate headed by billionaire Aga Khan, with Walter Swinburn in the saddle, passes the post to win The Derby by an astonishing record ten lengths, the longest in the race's 226 year history.

3rd June, 1981

Shergar was named European Horse of the Year 1981, after which he retired to Ballymany Stud, Ireland. He was kidnapped in 1983 by masked gunmen and a £2m ransom demanded. The owning syndicate refused to pay: *Shergar* was never seen again, nor were his abductors brought to justice.
1st September, 1981

Jockey Peter Scudamore, born in 1958 and trained with record breaking trainer Martin Pipe, rode 1,678 winners during his career and was Champion Jockey eight times.
30th October, 1981

Dick Saunders, riding *Grittar*, passes the winning post to win the 1982 Grand National and become the oldest winning jockey at 48. A farmer and amateur jockey, he was also Chairman of the Aintree Stewards and passionate about upholding Jockey Club rules. His experience allowed him to inject a note of caution to riders in the weighing room prior to the start of the demanding race.

3rd April, 1982

Geraldine Rees, on *Cheers*, storms on to finish eighth after negotiating The Chair. Rees became the first female jockey ever to finish the National.

3rd April, 1982

Graham Bradley rides *Bregawn* to win the Cheltenham Gold Cup. Born in 1960, Bradley courted controversy during his 12-year career as a jockey, receiving a two month suspension in 1982 for placing a bet while in the ring, then arrested and charged in 1999 in connection with race-fixing allegations, although the charges were dropped. Later he admitted in court to passing on 'sensitive racing information' to cocaine smuggler Brian Wright, who he met as a jockey in 1984.

17th March, 1983

Five horses from the Harewood stables of Michael Dickinson (foreground), that finished in the first five places in the 1983 Cheltenham Gold Cup: (L–R) *Silver Buck* (with stable lad Kevin Whyte), *Ashley House* (Steve Hardy), *Wayward Lad* (with head lad Brian Powell and George Foster), *Captain John* (Graham Rennison), and *Bregawn* (Jonathan Davies).
19th March, 1983

Corbiere, ridden by Ben
de Haan, comes home to
win the Grand National by
three-quarters of a length
from *Greasepaint*, ridden by
C Magnier.
9th April, 1983

Trainer Mrs Jenny Pitman, 37, welcomes Grand National winner *Corbiere* home with a kiss at the tiny Berkshire village of Upper Lambourn, after the long journey from Liverpool. *Corbiere* put Jenny into the record books as the first woman trainer of a National winner.

10th April, 1983

One of the world's greatest jockeys, Pat Eddery (L) with one of the foremost trainers in Europe, Vincent O'Brien. Eddery rode 4,632 British flat race winners, a figure bettered only by Sir Gordon Richards. He rode three winners of the Epsom Derby, and was Champion Jockey on eleven occasions, a record he shares with Lester Piggott.
31st May, 1983

A happy Willie Carson congratulates his horse, *Sun Princess*, after winning the Oaks Stakes at Epsom.

6th June, 1983

Hallo Dandy, Neil Doughty in the saddle (L), leads *Greasepaint*, ridden by Tommy Carmody, over the last fence before going on to win the Grand National, in the year that the most horses – 23 in number – finished the gruelling course.
31st March, 1984

Last Suspect (number 11), Hywel Davies in the saddle, clears
The Chair on his way to winning the Grand National as the
remainder of the field pour over the obstacle.
30th March, 1985

Facing page: The dramatic finish of the St Leger with the winner *Oh So Sharp*, ridden by Steve Cauthen (L) coming home ahead of *Lanfranco*, with Lester Piggot on board (R), in second place, and *Phardante*, ridden by Greville Starkey (C) in third place.

14th September, 1985

Lester Piggott, riding *Free Guest*, goes to the post for the last time before he retires as a jockey, at Newbury racecourse for the start of the St Simon Stakes. He finished second.

26th October, 1985

Stable girl Tina Gamlin with racehorse *The Liquidator,* in the indoor equine swimming pool at trainer Martin Pipe's lavish complex on the edge of Somerset's Blackdown Hills at Wellington.

16th February, 1986

Trainer Monica Dickinson with *Wayward Lad*, three times winner of the King George VI Chase. Sired by *Royal Highway* out of dam *Loughanmore*, he is owned by Shirley Thewlis and Les Abbott.

8th March, 1986

Dawn Run (R) ridden by
Jonjo O'Neill, leaping the
hurdle just in front of *Run
and Skip* (L), ridden by Steve
Smith-Eccles.
13th March, 1986

Dancing Brave, ridden by Pat Eddery, winning the King George VI and The Queen Elizabeth Diamond Stakes at Ascot, closely followed by *Shardari* ridden by Steve Cauthen.
26th July, 1986

Corbiere (R), previous National winner, with Ben de Haan on board, follows *Plundering* (second R), ridden by Peter Scudamore and *Why Forget* (L), Chris Grant in the saddle, over Becher's Brook in the Seagram Grand National at Aintree. The winner was *Maori Venture*.

4th April, 1987

The finish of the 1987 Derby, won by *Reference Point*, ridden by American jockey Steve Cauthen. In the US Cauthen, the 'Six Million Dollar Man', was the first jockey to win $6m in one season – his second year as a rider. In 1979, experiencing trouble making weight, he moved to England, where jockeys compete at lighter weights, and continued his successful career.
3rd June, 1987

The Henry Cecil-trained bay colt *Reference Point* is led into the winner's enclosure with Steve Cauthen aboard.
3rd June, 1987

Two picnicking racegoers in the back of a Land Rover, determined to sustain high spirits in the car park of a rainy Royal Ascot.
19th June, 1987

100 Years of Horse Racing • Twentieth Century in Pictures

Facing page: Stable lads from Lester Piggott's Eve Lodge stables bring three horses back from early morning exercises on the first day of their employer's three-year prison sentence, of which he served 366 days, for tax 'irregularities'. Piggott, stripped of the OBE awarded him in 1975, returned to jockeying in 1990, winning the Breeders' Cup Mile on *Royal Academy* and the 1992 2000 Guineas on *Rodrigo de Triano*. He officially retired in 1995.
24th October, 1987

Rhyme 'n' Reason (L), with Brendan Powell in the saddle, comes through to win from *Durham Edition* (R), ridden by Chris Grant, in the Grand National.
9th April, 1988

The grey gelding *Desert Orchid*, Simon Sherwood riding, races to a famous victory in the Cheltenham Gold Cup. The race was a mile longer than *Desert Orchid*'s believed preference, and rain and snow made the going heavier than he liked. *Racing Post* readers voted it the best horse race ever.

16th March, 1989

Facing page: Keen equestrian, competitor in the British eventing team and participant in the 1976 Olympic Games in Montreal, Princess Anne in action at Uttoxeter, Staffordshire.

22th April, 1989

A triumphant Willie Carson
aboard Derby winner
Nashwan, being led into the
winner's enclosure at the
Epsom Derby.
7th August, 1989

Jockey William Newnes on *Lots of Luck*, bringing up the rear in a shower of sand at Lingfield Park. It was the inaugural day of the racecourse's all weather track.

30th October, 1989

The binoculars that concealed an ultrasonic gun said to have been used to 'nobble' the horse *Il de Chypre*, leading in the King George V race at Royal Ascot on the 16th of June, 1988. The horse, second favourite, was seen to suddenly swerve, unseating its jockey Greville Starkey.
1st November, 1989

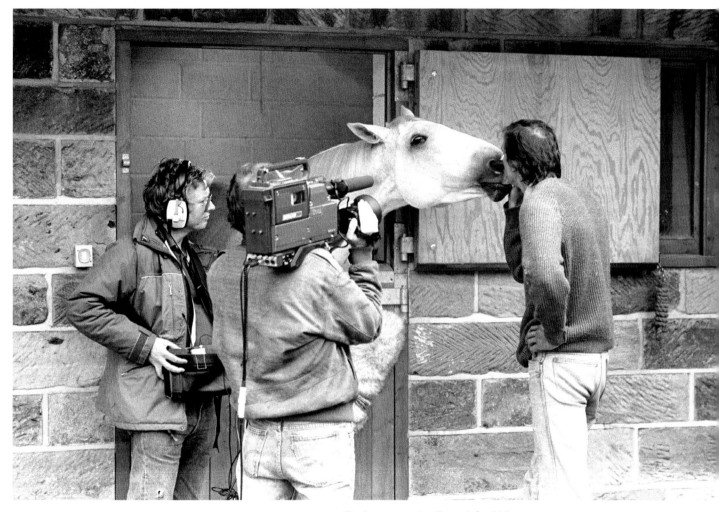

Equine superstar *Desert Orchid* at home in North Yorkshire gets a peck from owner Richard Burridge before the cameras – rolling for the horse's own television show.
8th December, 1989

Mr Frisk, ridden by Marcus
Armytage, is escorted back
to the paddock after winning
the Grand National.
7th April, 1990

Facing page: An artist paints
a picture of the Royal Ascot
paddock during the annual
summer event.
19th June, 1990

A spectacular jumper, *Desert Orchid* (second L) clears a fence in his final start of the season in the Cheltenham Gold Cup. In December 1991 the nation's favourite steeplechaser retired, although much of his time was spent raising money for charity and his fan club continued for 17 years.
14th March, 1991

Generous, with Alan Munro
in the saddle, powers past
the winning post to win the
Ever Ready Derby at Epsom.
5th June, 1991

Carl Llewellyn takes *Party Politics* past the finishing post to win the Grand National.
4th April, 1992

Following the second false start of the 1993 Grand National, one of the course stewards waves a red flag to stop the race at Aintree. Later, the race was declared void and was not re-run that year.

3rd April, 1993

The Queen, the Prince
of Wales and the Queen
Mother take a keen interest
in the day's proceedings at
The Derby, Epsom.
2nd June, 1993

A punter gets into the spirit
of the Epsom Derby.
3rd June, 1993

Intrepidity (L) with Michael Roberts on board winning the Energizer Oaks at Epsom from *Oakmead* (R) ridden by Frankie Dettori and *Royal Ballerina* (C) ridden by Warren O'Connor.

5th June, 1993

Richard Dunwoody crosses the finish on *Minnehoma* to win the Grand National.
9th April, 1994

Comedian Freddie Starr, whose passion is breeding and racing horses, was overjoyed when his horse *Minnehoma* won the 1994 Grand National.
10th April, 1994

Mister Baileys (C) with Jason Weaver in the saddle winning the Madagans 2,000 Guineas Stakes at Newmarket from *Grand Lodge* (L), ridden by Frankie Dettori.
30th April, 1994

The Ever Ready Derby field rounding Tattenham Corner,
with *Mister Baileys*, ridden by Jason Weaver, leading into the
straight and the eventual winner, *Erhaab*, (closest to rail, blue
and white striped hat) still in the chasing pack.
1st June, 1994

Facing page: The Queen
and Queen Mother watch
The Derby at Epsom.
1st June, 1994

Jockey Norman Williamson
with *Master Oats* after
winning the 1994 Coral
Welsh Grand National.
31st December, 1994

At Sedgefield Racecourse in County Durham, horses gallop through yellow fields of rape seed. The scene was less picturesque during the 2008 season, however, when the course suffered the highest animal casualty statistics in the country with 11 deaths in just over two weeks of racing.
5th May, 1995

Jamie Osborne falls from his horse *Black Humour* in a spectacular tumble during the Martell Cup at Aintree, breaking his collarbone in the accident.
28th March, 1996

A jubilant Frankie Dettori after leaping from *Mark of Esteem*, while still on the course, on winning the 2,000 Guineas at Newmarket.
4th May, 1996

The first woman to ride in The Derby, Alex Greaves, takes *Portugese Lil* out for a practice ride at Epsom racecourse before the big race. The following year, aged 36, she again made history as the first woman to ride a Group 1 winner when *Ya Malak* dead-heated in the 1997 Nunthorpe Stakes at York.

7th June, 1996

The exuberant Italian jockey Frankie Dettori celebrates on *Fujiyama Crest* after winning the last race at Ascot, the Gordon Carter Stakes. He won all seven races at Ascot, breaking the record.
28th September, 1996

The Prince of Wales talks with jockey Willie Carson, riding
Desert Orchid, during a parade of 50 horses and ponies
taking part in the launch of the British Horse Society's
Jubilee Year, at Buckingham Palace. The former Queen's
Jockey, who suffers from a recurrent back injury, was to
retire from racing.
5th February, 1997

Peter O'Sullevan at Aintree Racecourse, where he commentated on his 50th and final Grand National.
4th April, 1997

The crowds make their way
to an exit from the far side
of the Aintree course near
Canal Turn after a terrorist
bomb scare.
5th April, 1997

Disappointment for jockey
Robbie Supple, who sits
behind the first Grand
National fence as the crowd
stream out after the race
was abandoned following a
bomb scare.
5th April, 1997

Grand National horses find
a new home in the stables
at Haydock Park after a
terrorist scare.
6th April, 1997

Overjoyed and exhausted, jockey Tony Dobbin hugs the neck of his mount, *Lord Gyllene,* after the pair had won the Grand National.

7th April, 1997

Tote Cheltenham Gold
Cup winner, *Cool Dawn*
ridden by Andrew Thornton
(foreground).
19th March, 1998

At the Martel Grand National, eventual winner Carl Llewellyn on *Earth Summit* (R) leads the field at Canal Turn from Gordon Shenkin, on *Maple Dancer* (L).
4th April, 1998

Jockey Frankie Dettori kisses the Queen Mother's hand after she presented him with the London Clubs Trophy for the leading rider at Ascot. The Italian had amassed an impressive seven victories over the four days of the Royal Meeting.
20th June, 1998

Facing page: Jockey Daryll Holland (C) salutes his horse *Double Trigger* as he wins the Doncaster Cup for the third time at Doncaster races. The following year *Double Trigger* was honoured by having a Great North Eastern Railway train named after him. GNER, which sponsors the Doncaster Cup, was marking the horse's historic third success in the race.
10th September, 1998

Paul Carbury (C) goes over
Canal Turn on his way to
winning the Martell Grand
National on *Bobbyjo*, behind
Feels Like Gold.
10th April, 1999

Frankie Dettori crosses the line to win the 2,000 Guineas at Newmarket on *Island Sands*.
1st May, 1999

Frankie Dettori leaps with delight off his mount, *Daylami*, after winning the King George VI and Queen Elizabeth Diamond Stakes, at Ascot. The Italian rider was renowned for such 'flying dismounts'.
24th July, 1999

Hats out in full force at
Glorious Goodwood, as
spectators watch the racing.
29th July, 1999

The irrepressible Frankie Dettori leaps from the saddle of *Dubai Millennium* after winning the Queen Elizabeth II Stakes at Ascot. The race was due to be run on the Saturday, but the first day of Ascot Festival was cancelled due to rain and a waterlogged course.

26th September, 1999

Tony McCoy celebrates after gaining his 1,000th career win on *Majadou* in the Wragge and Co. Handicap Chase at Chellenham.

11th December, 1999

Facing page: Jockey Ruby Walsh, riding horse *Papillon* (C), on their way to winning the Martell Grand National. Walsh, reigning Irish National Hunt champion in 2009, is the son of *Papillon's* trainer, the former champion amateur jockey Ted Walsh.
8th April, 2000

Charlie Swan and horse *Istabraq*, celebrating their third consecutive Smurfit Champion Hurdle win at Cheltenham.
14th March, 2000

Best Mate, ridden by Jim Culloty, clears the last fence on his way to a third consecutive Cheltenham Gold Cup victory.
18th March, 2004

The dust flies as runners and riders jump a fence during the Cheltenham Better Value Odds Skybet Handicap Steeple Chase.
14th March, 2005

Kicking King cools off after winning the Totesport Cheltenham Gold Cup.
18th March, 2005

RED RUM'S
GRAVE

←

Please Remain On
This Side Of The
Running Rail

One of the horses scheduled
to compete in the day's
Grand National completes
its morning exercise on the
gallops, passing the grave of
Red Rum.
6th April, 2005

Grey Abbey and jockey Graham Lee (foreground) beat *First Gold* and jockey Tony McCoy to win the Betfair Bowl, a Grade 2 National Hunt chase for horses five years old and above, run over three miles one furlong at Aintree Racecourse during the John Smith's Grand National meeting.

7th April, 2005

Trainer Henrietta Knight (L) and jockey Paul Carberry look on after racehorse *Best Mate* collapsed during the William Hill Haldon Gold Cup Chase at Exeter. The triple Cheltenham Gold Cup winner died after suffering a suspected heart attack. Knight said: *"I was actually on the track where he came down and I was the first one there. I knew immediately he had died."*
1st November, 2005

Racegoers await the best
dressed competition.
7th April, 2006

Paddy Brennan on *Inglis Drever* celebrates winning the Ladbroke World Hurdle, at the Cheltenham three day festival.

15th March, 2007

Facing page: *Point Barrow*, the favourite for the Grand National, falls at the first fence with jockey Phillip Carberry.
14th April, 2007

Finsceal Beo ridden by jockey Kevin Manning, on their way to winning the Stan James 1,000 Guineas Stakes at Newmarket Racecourse.
6th May, 2007

Notnowcato ridden by Ryan Moore (second L) edges home to win The Coral Eclipse from *Authorized* (L) ridden by Frankie Dettori.
7th July, 2007

Facing page: *Pass It On* swims in the pool during a visit to Jonjo O'Neill's stables at Jackdaws Castle, Temple Guiting, Gloucestershire.
15th October, 2007

Eventual winner *Miko De Beauchene*, ridden by Andrew Thornton, chases second placed *Halcon Generlardais*, ridden by Christian Williams, along the finishing straight at the Coral Welsh National at Chepstow.
27th December, 2007

A TV cameraman takes
evasive action as a loose
horse breaks through the rail
at Newbury.
29th December, 2007

Kauto Star with stable hand Sonja Warburton at Paul Nicholls' Stables in Ditcheat, Somerset.
20th February, 2008

Trainer Paul Nicholls with
the Cheltenham Gold Cup
and his trio of winners, (L–R)
Kauto Star, Denman and
Neptune Collonges, during
a parade around Ditcheat,
Somerset.
15th March, 2008

Timmy Murphy celebrates
his victory on *Comply or Die*
in the John Smith's Grand
National Handicap Chase,
part of the Grand National
Meeting at Aintree.
5th April, 2008

Channel 4 racing pundit
John McCririck.
6th June, 2008

Facing page: A close up
of the horses' hooves
during the SkyBet.com
Bobby Renton Handicap
Steeplechase, supporting
spinal research.
15th October, 2008

Spare Me, ridden by
Dutchman Tjade Collier,
on his way to winning the
Legsby Road Claiming
Hurdle at Market Rasen,
Lincolnshire.
20th November, 2008

Jockey Tony McCoy (R) talks to trainer Nicky Henderson after finishing seventh on *Excape* in the Weatherbys Bank Juvenile Novices' Hurdle at Plumpton.
9th February, 2009